Defeating Communism One More Time

~ Using the "good" of Cyberspace to Stop Chinese Global Aggression

Mark A. Russo

Former Chief Information Security Officer
for the Department of Education

Syber-Risk

DEDICATION

This book is dedicated to my supportive instructors and professors at the National Defense University, Washington, DC, and their daily efforts to train and teach the next generation of cyber-warriors of this great Nation.

This essay is also dedicated to my family, who have been supportive of my endeavors to plunge into writing as not just a hobby but a calling to make the world a better and more secure place.

Defeating Communism One More Time

by Mark A. Russo

Printed in the United States of America.

September 2019:

Revision History for the
First Edition
First Release

ABSTRACT

While the Trump Administration has recruited some of the best (and controversial) minds in fighting global terrorism, it has yet to identify and recruit experts with the credentials to defeat threats to the US and its allies in cyberspace. The Chinese cyber threat is the #1 menace in the domain of cyberspace as well as Russia, Iran, and North Korea. While the US was historically focused on the former Soviet Union, i.e., Russia, and more recently in the physical world, the threat of radical jihadist terrorism, the Chinese have grown economically, technologically, militarily, and politically to pose the gravest threat to US cyber interests. The solution to defeating Chinese cyber operations may be found in the leveraging the Administration's counter-terror expertise and applying principles from seasoned experts to thwart and defeat government-sponsored Chinese hackers. The solution will more be found in active use of "soft cyber power" (SCP), which is primarily information dominance focused, AND "hard-cyber power" (HCP), which will be the more comprehensive solution to defeating Chinese supremacy in cyberspace.

Defeating Communism One More Time

TABLE OF CONTENTS

CISCO'S® SURVIVAL IN THE "AGE OF CHINA."

For anyone who works actively within the Information Technology (IT) arena, the company synonymous with the Internet's backend infrastructure is Cisco ® Systems. It produces most of the world's major infrastructure hardware devices, such as firewalls, routers, and bridges. These devices are critical to the creation and maintenance of the global Internet.

Even after the "dot-com" burst of 1997-2003 (Business Insider, 2010), it recovered exceptionally and has continued to be a significant manufacturer of critical network devices found as the foundational elements of most of any company's IT network. "As of [2018], Cisco® generates revenues of over $49 billion and has dominant positions in 18 different IT product lines" (Taulli, 2018). Cisco's® post "dot-com" bubble success can be attributed directly to Cisco's senior leadership and its strategy that ensured its long-term ability to remain competitive and profitable.

Strategic Leadership Focus

There are many sources (McGregor, 2018; Swartz, 2018; Taulli, 2018) that place the direct and current success of Cisco on recently retired, Chief Executive Officer John Chambers. It was his strategic leadership that ensured Cisco's long-term viability in a highly-specialized segment of the IT marketplace. Three essential strategies can enumerate Chamber's approach: "...find ways to innovate to scale, build a culture that is focused on the needs of the customer and develop a flexible network infrastructure [for its customers]" (Taulli, 2018). These strategies continue to support its market profitability with a current corporate valuation of $216 billion (Swartz, 2018).

"Strategic leadership is about how to most effectively manage a company's strategy-making process to create a competitive advantage" (Hill, Schilling, & Jones, 2017). Chamber's three tenets do precisely that. They provide the vision and focus on creating a shared understanding of leadership's approach to creating a competitive position in the market. Tenet one, "innovating to scale," understands that no one device can be applied equally across differing markets, for example, medical, business, finance, and especially small business; cost concerns and capability are a vital concern for any segment of the industry. "Focusing on the needs of the customer" directly supports the first tenet; if you do not understand the variability across the customer base, it may result in lost revenues in specific markets that do not feel their needs are adequately being met by the products produced. Finally, developing "flexible network options" also reinforces the primary strategy. Cisco has not only implemented a strong and mutually supportive strategy for its competitiveness but has sustained its leadership position based upon its continuing primacy in the IT back-end hardware environment.

Analysis of Cisco's® Internal and External Factors

The most common approach to analyzing internal and external factors impacting how Cisco® has managed its long-term competitiveness is by using a Strengths-Weaknesses- Opportunities-Threat (SWOT) analysis. While the actual analysis is typically restricted, and not accessible in the public domain, there are many SWOT analyses done from the complex to the basic. Washburn University accomplished an uncomplicated analysis in 2016 that can be found in Figure 1.

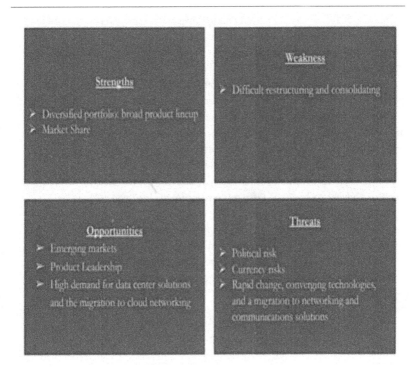

Figure 1. Cisco® SWOT Analysis. Adapted from "Cisco" by A. Boyd, B. Smith, D.M. Poletti, S. Specht, 2016, Washburn University, p. 23. No Copyright 2016 by Washburn University.

The internal analysis begins with a review of a company's resources, capabilities, and competencies (Hill, Schilling, & Jones, 2017). These are typically identified in a SWOT analysis by the strengths and weaknesses quadrants specific to its internal operations. As suggested in Figure 1, a critical internal strength can be found in its capabilities to include a diversified product line that does not only include network hardware devices.

In 2017, software accounted for 22% of Cisco's® overall revenues (Morningstar, 2018). This strength continues to be a focus in 2019 because of the ongoing commercial demands for specialized software in the IT back office management area. Cisco's® focus on software remains a vital part of its ability to anticipate and to attempt to lead

(Chambers, 2015) through such transitions, for example, ongoing volatility in the data center development market. It is this strength that Cisco continues to align with its founding strategies to innovate and focus on the needs of the customer, and to ensure its continuing profitability.

The opportunities and threats quadrants of a SWOT analysis help to derive external environmental factors impacting profits. Morningstar analysis (Morningstar, 2018) of Cisco Systems recognizes that its significant opportunity for continued profitability relies upon its brand loyalty. This loyalty factor is very high, and customers recognize that switching costs to other vendors are risky and cost-prohibitive.

Cisco® would also conduct its external analysis based upon Porter's *Five Forces model* (Hill, Schilling, & Jones, 2017). The "bargaining power of buyers" provides a significant advantage to Cisco. Cisco recognizes that the back-end network infrastructure community is "…inherently risk-averse…" (Morningstar, 2018, p. 2), and have leveraged this understanding where it can charge premium prices based upon it; changes in equipment may have unforeseen impacts on customer operations, and many of the current Cisco-based infrastructure companies are not willing to make decisions that affect their profitability.

The sample, Figure 1, SWOT analysis, is necessary for its consideration of economic threats to any company. Political and currency risks are common risks. They are the "known-knowns" of risk. These are universal risks when selling goods and services in global markets with different economies and political structures.

A significant flaw not anticipated by Porter (Hill, Schilling, & Jones, 2017) is **economic espionage** and its impacts on markets. Nowhere can that be seen more dramatically is the brazen and continued spying efforts by China. In 2019, federal prosecutors were pursuing criminal investigations of Chinese companies stealing trade secrets from both the U.S. and its trading partners (Hong, Strumpf, & Viswantha, 2019). It is an imbalance of rivalries among companies that have access to a nation-state political and intelligence apparatus. Cisco®, as well as its competitors, faces an extra-daunting task to compete fairly in the global market; China is a specific threat of the Twenty-first Century not addressed, for example, by Porter.

Additionally, such an external threat not only poses challenges to the market but the entire IT supply chain. In February 2015, the Director of National Intelligence (DNI), identified one of the significant risks facing the United States (U.S.) within the "Cyber" domain is the insertion of malicious code into IT hardware and software items sold to the U.S. According to the DNI: "Despite ever-improving network defenses, the diverse possibilities for...supply chain operations to insert compromised hardware or software...will hold nearly all [Information and Communication Technology] systems at risk for years to come" (Director of National Intelligence, 2015, p. 1).

While several foreign IT equipment and software companies have been accused of such activities, the primary threat in this arena is the Chinese company *Huawei (Wah-way) Technologies Company, Limited*. In 2012, the House Permanent Select Committee on Intelligence had significant concerns. Specific to its investigation of the operating practices of Huawei, the committee reported that: "The threat posed [by Huawei/China] to U.S. national-security interests... in the telecommunications supply chain is an increasing priority..." (U.S. House of Representatives, 2012, p. 1).

Huawei represents a similar and more pervasive threat to the international IT supply chain and creates an even higher risk to Cisco® and others like market competitors. Huawei has both the means and motives to compromise IT equipment and systems on behalf of the Chinese government. Furthermore, Huawei has refused to explain its relationship with the Chinese government or the role of the Chinese Communist Party (Simonite, 2012), and it can be assumed, based on multiple Huawei senior leaders with close ties with the People's Liberation Army (PLA), that Huawei has an explicit connection with the Chinese government.

Porter did not consider how corporate espionage may impact the overall success of a company. He did not consider or anticipate the massive resources of a nation are applied to overwhelm it in the global marketplace. China, as a macro-threat in the marketplace, should be additionally considered as well as other dictatorial governments with capabilities to exploit the Internet as has China over many years.

The success of a company to both sustain its operations and maintain its profitability is a matter of good leadership. Leaders, such as Cisco's John Chambers, have proven to be significant in ensuring Cisco's® profitability. He understood that the ability to anticipate, capture, and lead through market transitions (Chambers, 2015) are vital to the success and solvency of a company. It was due to his focus on a well-designed and articulated strategic leadership approach that ensures Cisco's® ongoing success. His tenacity to face the daily and daunting challenges of global cyber-threats may be one way to fight these threats successfully—but there may be other solutions as well.

References

Business Insider. (2010, December 15). *Here's why the dot com bubble began and why it popped.* Retrieved from Business Insider: https://www.businessinsider.com/heres-why-the-dot-com-bubble-began-and-why-it-popped-2010-12

Chambers, J. (2015, May). *Cisco's CEO on staying ahead of technology shifts.* Retrieved from Harvard business review: https://hbr.org/2015/05/ciscos-ceo-on-staying-ahead-of-technology-shifts

Director of National Intelligence. (2015, February 26). *Statement of record: Worldwide threat assessment.* Retrieved from http://www.armed-services.senate.gov/imo/media/doc/Stewart_02-26-15.pdf

Hill, C. W., Schilling, M. A., & Jones, G. R. (2017). *Strategic management: An integrated approach: theory & cases.* Boston: Cengage learning.

Hong, N., Strumpf, D., & Viswantha, A. (2019, January 16). *Huawei targeted in U.S. criminal probe for alleged theft of trade secrets.* Retrieved from Wall street journal: https://www.wsj.com/articles/federal-prosecutors-pursuing-criminal-case-against-huawei-for-alleged-theft-of-trade-secrets-11547670341

McGregor, J. (2018, September 14). *Former Cisco CEO John Chambers wants to make America a start-up nation again.* Retrieved from Washington post: https://www.washingtonpost.com/business/2018/09/14/former-cisco-ceo-john-chambers-wants-make-america-start-up-nation-again/?utm_term=.5660202edf72

Morningstar. (2018, November 15). *Cisco systems inc.* Retrieved from Morningstar Investment Research database

Simonite, T. (2012, October 9). *Why the United States is so afraid of Huawei?* Retrieved from MIT technology review: http://www.technologyreview.com/news/429542/why-the-united-states-is-so-afraid-of-huawei/

Swartz, J. (2018, August 23). *After Cisco, John Chambers is still dreaming big about tech.* Retrieved from Barron's: https://www.barrons.com/articles/after-cisco-john-chambers-is-still-dreaming-big-about-tech-1535046077

Taulli, T. (2018, October 20). *Leadership lessons from cisco's john chambers.* Retrieved from Forbes: https://www.forbes.com/sites/tomtaulli/2018/10/20/leadership-lessons-from-ciscos-john-chambers/#2d202e8a4240

U.S. House of Representatives. (2012, October 8). *Investigative report on the US national security issues posed by Chinese telecommunications companies Huawei and ZTE.* Retrieved from https://intelligence.house.gov/sites/intelligence.house.gov/files/documents/Huawei-ZTE%20Investigative%20Report%20(FINAL).pdf

THE CHINA THREAT

The Mandiant Report

Even with substantive evidence of Chinese Cyber Operations (CO) against the US, they have consistently deflected any evidence brought to the public. Seemingly, Chinese government hackers have been unconcerned with their identities and attribution "fingerprints" found by computer forensic investigators. Their lack of concern regarding *attribution*[1], for example, of their CO activities raises the question of their stability and potential escalation that may be a future step if provoked. It highlights an apparent danger of their possible use of more overt military/kinetic responses *and* CO in an impending attack.

The 2013 *Mandiant Report* exhaustively provided evidence *traceable* to mainland China. The report identified in "...over 97% of the 1,905 times Mandiant observed Advanced

> **MANDIANT REPORT CONCLUSION:**
> "The sheer scale and duration of sustained attacks against such a wide set of industries from a singularly identified group based in China leaves little doubt about the organization behind APT1,"
> (Mandiant, 2013, p. 6).

Persistent Threat 1 (APT) 1 [Chinese] intruders connecting to their attack infrastructure, [and] APT 1 used [Internet Protocol] IP addresses registered in Shanghai and systems set to use the Simplified Chinese language," (Mandiant, 2013, p. 4). Additionally, "817 of the 832 (98%) IP addresses logging into APT1 controlled systems using Remote Desktop resolved back to China" (Ibid.). This lack of concern by the Chinese of evidentiary and legal indictments suggests they have no desire to keep their ambitions completely

---

[1] "*Attribution* means knowing who is attacking you, and being able to respond appropriately against the actual place that the attack is originating from," (Keys, Winstead, & Simmons, 2010).

secret--and that makes them even more dangerous.

The 2013 *Mandiant Report, APT 1: Exposing One of China's Cyber Espionage Units,* demonstrates the most evident danger posed by China. This report is the hallmark of open-source attribution against the Chinese government and its CO; however, the Chinese remain committed to ignoring such findings and subjecting the West to a narrative that these findings are not conclusive proof of any action by China.

In 2015, Chinese President Xi continued such denials of wrongdoing during a *Wall Street Journal* interview: "The Chinese government does not engage in theft of commercial secrets in any form, nor does it encourage or support Chinese companies to engage in such practices in any way," (Collins, 2015). However, it continues CO against the US while they publicly counter allegations of factual findings regarding Chinese government-sponsored hacking. The US should expect Chinese leadership will continue to direct and condone such actions in cyberspace with the permission and full support of this significant nation-state.

Congressional Concerns

The threat extends beyond hacking activities and typical efforts by nation-states to engage in cyber espionage as an extension of any states' typical spying activities. For China, this includes entry into the global Information Technology (IT) supply chain. These include vital hardware components such as computers, firewalls, routers, switches, etc. The danger and the concern regarding Chinese economic activities include the potential to introduce IT products that may be compromised by malicious code that allows unauthorized access to systems and networks. It is China's expanded entry into the IT hardware sector that further demonstrates China's inherent capability to gain access to US public and private computer systems surreptitiously.

China's ability to use its economic and technologic entities includes major Chinese-owned IT companies to include Lenovo, ZTE, and Huawei. These corporations have become international powerhouses in the IT product markets. In 2012, the House Permanent Select Committee on Intelligence (HPSCI) had significant concerns regarding China's ability to infiltrate the world's IT supply chain. Specific to its investigation of the operating practices of Huawei, the committee reported that: "The threat posed [by China] to U.S. national-security interests... in the telecommunications supply chain is an increasing priority..." (US House of Representatives, 2012, p.1). The fear continues to be that the Chinese access into the free market has also brought dangers to both private and public sector network operations via the supply chain.

The 2012 HPSCI investigation provided no conclusive finding of an introduction of malicious code or viruses into commercial Chinese IT products in 2006; however, a discrete prohibition by several Western nations, to include the US, was initiated against Lenovo Personal Computers. The use or purchase of Lenovo PCs "...due to backdoor vulnerabilities" (Infosec Institute, 2013) was banned. Concerns still exist about how China *also* poses a threat to the international IT supply chain. It has the explicit means to compromise IT hardware, equipment, and systems globally.

The US Begins to Get Serious

China's economic cyber espionage growth has been a concern for current and past Administrations. In 2013, the National Security Advisor for President Obama raised worries about the rampant threat posed by China in its activities against the US. During a speech to the Asia Society on Manhatten's Upper East Side, he expressed concerns "...about sophisticated, targeted theft of business information and proprietary technologies through cyber intrusions emanating from China," (Kaplan, 2016, p. 221). This was the first public denunciation of Chinese CO by an Administration. It was during this period that the US openly and publicly brought national concern regarding Chinese warfare activities into the public domain.

The following year, the Federal Bureau of Investigation (FBI) announced the indictment of 5 People's Liberation Army officers identified for hacking US computer systems. This was the first substantive time an Administration used law enforcement as a mechanism to identify cyber espionage attributed by US intelligence and law enforcement activities and to levy charges against agents of a foreign power. It was this action that formally and openly placed China "on notice." Unfortunately, no other follow-on actions were pursued, and the fate of US cybersecurity was passed to the next Administration.

A NEW DIRECTION

The current Administration has recruited the top thinkers and planners to fight the scourge of global terrorism, focusing primarily on the physical manifestation of the Islamic State in Iraq and Syria (ISIS); however, it has yet to recruit the "A-team" to fight and win the ongoing battles in cyberspace. Experts, such as Dr. Sebastian Gorka, are thought-leaders who have actively focused upon strategic efforts within the Administration to address the threat posed by global terror. *So, why can't the US use the same ideas and principles of fighting terrorism to defeat the varied vestiges of Chinese cyber warfare?*

This essay analyzes the current Administration's potential approach to defeating terrorism and how it may be extrapolated to fighting active Chinese Cyber Operations (CO)[2] targeting the US, and its application to other significant cyber-threats to include Russia, Iran, and North Korea. It is intended to provide a recommended framework of actions and solutions to not only deter and dissuade but to defeat a Chinese cyber onslaught specifically; a threat aimed at abolishing the US and its core ideology similarly as radical jihadists seek to the destroy the US in the physical world.

US Congressman Mike Rogers stated that: "China's economic espionage has reached an intolerable level, and … that the United States and our allies in Europe and Asia must confront Beijing and demand that they put a stop to this piracy," (Mandiant, 2013).

---

[2] "CO can deliver unique capabilities and combat power through cyberspace, but the US military does not act in a unified manner when conducting these operations, especially when acting in concert with other warfighting functions," (Applegate, Carpenter, & West, 2017).

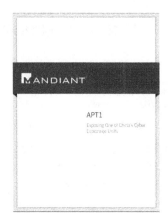

Mandiant's 2013 Report on Advanced Persistent Threat 1 →
China [People's Liberation Army (PLA) Unit 61398]

This danger to the US is the most significant national security threat in the virtual combat space; it requires constant vigilance and continuous monitoring. Bill Gertz states in his book, *iWar*, that "...China represents the greatest long-term threat to American national interests" (Gertz, 2017). While ISIS poses a direct physical threat to the US and global community interests, the Chinese and its primary cyber-projection unit, PLA Unit 61398, poses the greatest threat in cyberspace; a threat that has been allowed to expand without checks to its growing international power.

Synopsis of PLA Unit 61398

The evidence we have collected on PLA Unit 61398's mission and infrastructure reveals an organization that:

» Employs hundreds, perhaps thousands of personnel

» Requires personnel trained in computer security and computer network operations

» Requires personnel proficient in the English language

» Has large-scale infrastructure and facilities in the "Pudong New Area" of Shanghai

» Was the beneficiary of special fiber optic communication infrastructure provided by state-owned enterprise China Telecom in the name of national defense

(Mandiant's 2013 Report, p. 19)

The Chinese cyber-threat is the most pervasive. China's broad capabilities to conduct CO, their likely exfiltration of millions of personnel records from the Office of Personnel Management in June 2015, and theft of US sensitive technologic and corporate intellectual property, demonstrates a lack of concern about current US counter-offensive responses. The US needs to halt the Chinese through a deliberate and "offensive" blueprint of action. Such a plan must marginalize and dissuade, deter, and ultimately defeat Chinese ambitions and convey US ideas directly to the average Chinese citizen. This can be done effectively through the power of technology and the interconnected communications of the current-day Internet. It also must employ the same technologies to monitor Chinese and other nation-state actors in cyberspace. (Also, see Appendix B on its discussion about "Continuous Monitoring").

Distracted

Historically, the US was focused on the overall threat posed by the former Soviet Union, which aided an unimpeded growth of China into the 21sy Century. It was this early distraction that helped China begin its rise. More recently, the US was engrossed with the multitude of increased global terrorist factions, such as Al Qaeda, the Taliban, and the expansionist successes of ISIS in the Middle East. China emerged as a "superpower" during this period of tumult and chaos; the US failed to stifle Chinese global and technological ambitions where it had formerly and successfully contained the Soviet Union to the point of dissolution; China has become the most inimitable threat to cyberspace due in large part to the US's averted focus on other presumed more significant threats to US national security concerns.

Also, some experts on China contributed for many years to create a false sense of security for US leadership regarding China's ambitions to become a global superpower. Analysis by some academics suggested that: "China [was] too bogged down in the security challenges within and around its borders to threaten the West **unless the West weakens itself to the point of creating a power vacuum** [emphasis added]," (Andrew & Scobell, 2012, p. xi), contributed further to the US's averted attention. The US allowed a *void* as foretold to occur. This was a contributing national security failure. The US did not recognize the long-term threat posed by China.

The belief about China's inability to challenge the West occurred because of poor analysis that they could not protect its large and continuous borders. It was this wrong belief that China could only "worry about its own domestic challenges" posed by its borders, (Andrew & Scobell, 2012) contributed to its accelerated political and technological growth in the 21st Century. The failure of multiple Administrations to expect and to act against China's solidification of its power was a failure of both political parties and their experts who failed to prepare for this significant shift in global power.

As suggested by Andrew and Scobell's analysis, (Andrew & Scobell, 2012), it was also due in part to the lack of understanding by US leadership of the more significant challenges created by an interconnected and technological world; the US failed to recognize China's embrace and use of technology as part of its desire to be a significant world power. Experts, academics, and politicians contributed to this diversion that created the vacuum that China so desperately needed; it was *easier* to focus on more tangible and physical world threats such as ISIS and Al Qaeda than to understand how the World Wide Web would become so vital to China's global and technical aspirations.

The US had done little until recently to dissuade China in the realm of CO. China has taken full advantage of the years of US distraction. The threat accelerated under the advent of cyberspace, and now, they have become significant leaders in cyberspace. China is fully capable of conducting explicit CO against the world and the US, specifically.

COUNTER-TERROR TACTICS

The Trump Administration has yet to name any significant cybersecurity "experts" to its national security structure. While the former mayor of New York City, Rudolph Giuliani, a former White House "Cybersecurity Advisor," he and several lawyers have been brought into the Administration with less-than-adequate technical knowledge to conduct strategic defensive or offensive planning and execution. This includes the designation of the new Chief of Staff for the Department of Homeland Security (DHS)[3] , who is identified as a cybersecurity expert. She has little substantive technical or cyber managerial experience to direct DHS efforts in the non-Department of Defense (DOD) area of responsibility. The necessity for cybersecurity professionals is critical to bolstering the Administration's commitment to focus real proficiencies to fighting Chinese aspirations.

An additional concern is that while these individuals have good cyber policy experience, in terms of cybersecurity technical credentials, they are genuinely trivial choices. Rudolph Giuliani[4] has an extensive legal, political, and law enforcement

---

[3] Kirstjen Nielsen named the current DHS Chief of Staff. Her most significant credentials include serving for 6 years as a senior fellow of the Resilience Task Force at the George Washington University's (GWU) Center for Cyber and Homeland Security. She has is characterized as a "policy wonk."
[4] Mayor Giuliani was a key and fateful figure that led a nation through the period after the attacks of 9/11 in NYC.

background; however, neither he nor his security companies, Giuliani Security LLC, are considered significant cybersecurity entities such as Fire Eye®, Fortinet®, Mandiant® or even Cisco Systems®. *So, where will the core leadership arise to counter the Chinese cyber threat?*

A likely orchestrator of the current Administration's cybersecurity efforts may include a relatively astute, but some-what controversial assistant to the president, Dr. Sebastian Gorka. Dr. Gorka has credentials working with past Administrations and has been a regular lecturer for the US Special Operations Command specific to the challenges of combating international terrorism. He has several publications and positions on how best to address the terror threat. He stated in a 2017 interview with *Fox Business News* that "...the real threat in terms of cyber is China" (Gorka S., 2017).

Gorka's core solution, in terms of countering terrorism, concentrated on working with moderate Muslim countries and employing "soft" power solutions to include specifically Information Operations (IO). Based on his writings, (Gorka S. L., 2016), such approaches seem a rational solution even though contrary portrayals by significant news outlets describe Dr. Gorka's methods as "fringe,[5]" (Jaffe, 2017). He had the requisite knowledge, background, and access to key members of the Administration to help to develop a needed strategy. He was positioned within the Administration to boost the US's ability to counter ongoing Chinese cyber efforts.

In his book, *Defeating Jihad*, Dr. Gorka espoused that the "...next president must start a strategic-level counterpropaganda campaign from inside the National Security Council..." (Gorka, 2016).[6] *What if the same type of campaign was waged against the Chinese?* Defeating the Chinese will not require armed conflict, but a battle of ideas and competing ideologies to eliminate the Chinese cyber threat.

---

[5] Dr. Gorka is part of a tumultuous time in the US's political history; however, to describe "working with moderate Muslim countries" as fringe or radical makes no sense by any interpretation.
[6] Dr. Gorka published his book in April 2016 with little expectation of being in a key national security role in 2017.

The Most "Evil of Empires"

It was President Reagan's rhetoric regarding "the evil empire" that created an effective first-step in an IO campaign in the 1980s, and the associated substantive growth of US military that sped the Soviet Union to its ultimate defeat.[7] It was not due to the US's physical/military power engaging the Soviets on the battlefield, but the commitment, expression, and demonstration of the idea of US preeminence that caused Moscow to crumble. It was a strategic IO plan established at the US's highest national security level, to include the president, that eroded the Soviet Union's ability to be a further threat to the US. *Why cannot alike commitment overmatch Chinese cyber aspirations result in a like defeat?*

A Defunct Ideology

The currently sought tenets of counter-terrorism action can also be applied against the Chinese as well as the other significant cyber-actors and threats: 1) "deploy the truth," and 2) "help others fight their wars," (Gorka, 2016). This strategic concept could be employed by the Administration firmly and resolutely. Any messaging must be truthful about the competing ideologies of capitalism and the failed form of Chinese communism. It will require the US and its partners to isolate China ideologically and to defeat it using the global community.

Dr. Gorka could still play a key role in defeating China substantively in a war of ideas in cyberspace. The same conceptual approach that he presents in terms of the terrorist threat is the use and employment of an active "counter-propaganda" campaign as the core strategy against Chinese cyber-attacks, (Gorka, 2017). The use of specific SCP

---

[7] If such strategic operations are to be truly effective, they must not only include the identification of the threat publicly, but apply all elements of power: Diplomatic, Informational, Military, and Economic (DIME) to have a successful plan.

solutions, not requiring kinetic or para-kinetic effects[8], is a better approach to defeating China.

---

[8] P*ara-kinetic effects* in cyberspace have physical-like impacts on IT equipment such as routers, switches, and firewalls. Usually not considered "acts of war," they may include a Denial of Service (DOS) attack or manipulation of data to include deletion, modification, or exfiltration.

THE BLUEPRINT

Shift to the Offense

Before discussing strategies and more specific tactics to defeat the Chinese, the US must move beyond the outdated approach of being on the defense. The US can no longer maintain a sense of futility. In January 2013, a task force within the Defense Science Board "...concluded that there was no reliable defense against a resourceful, dedicated cyber attacker" (Kaplan, 2016, p. 275). The US can no longer maintain a defeatist point of view. ***It must go on the offense***.

The first component of defeating the Chinese requires US leadership committed to offensive SCP operations in cyberspace just as it is focused on similar actions against ISIS. The *National Military Strategy for Cyber Operations* expressed this point of view: "...the need for "offensive capabilities in cyberspace [are necessary] to gain and maintain the initiative," (Kaplan, 2016, p. 211). It is time to address the threats posed by Chinese CO. The expectation is that the new national security leadership team will employ offensive operations, more specifically, the use of SCP actions.[9] Such activities would exploit social media, technologies, and classic military principles of IO.

---

[9] From the "range of cyber options," it is expected that there will be the use of kinetic options; however, it is expected a greater reliance of SCP actions, that involve human psychology, and expanded use of all available means of social media in cyberspace. (See Figure 1).

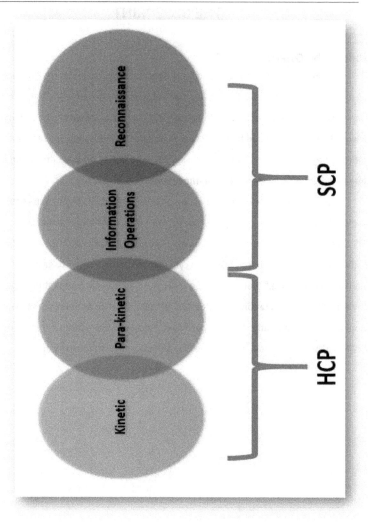

Figure 1. Range of Cyber Options

Any Administration should be committed to defeating global terrorism, and must also express a real commitment to defeating the Chinese on the cyber-terrain of virtual space. New leaders in counter-terrorism will likely not seek direct military confrontations in the physical world; they will seek effective information operations to defeat the Chinese. General Joseph Votel, the current commander of US Central Command, about the coordinated need for State Department support, stated: "the short answer is no, we cannot [win the war without soft power]," (Houck, 2017). This should include a focus on denouncing the failure of the communist ideology and the adverse impacts on the average Chinese citizen.

Voice of America 2.0 – Disruptive Technology

Bill Gertz, in his book, *iWar: War and Peace in the Information Age,* outlined a "...information warfare strategy to mitigate the [cyber] threats" (Gertz, 2017). His overall approach toward worldwide cyber actors, to include China, relies on SCP. His tactic is about returning US information operation dominance as a significant solution to capturing the "hearts and minds" of the enemy. He suggested the reinvigoration of the US Information Agency (USIA) which its most notable role was broadcasting unbiased communication to varied global totalitarian nations under the name of "Voice of America" --it was abolished in 1999.

The creation of a strategic next-step technical solution is called *Voice of America 2.0 (VOA 2.0)*

VOA 2.0 is an advanced and disruptive technological solution. It is the "first pillar" of defeating Chinese CO. (See Figure 2, "The Three Pillars"). This component is a significant part of the strategic approach that supports the overall effort to weaken Chinese leadership's control of information dissemination to its citizenry. It is intended to provide unfettered access to the Internet and bypass dictatorial nations from interference by its censors or blocking technologies.

VOA 2.0 would provide global high-speed satellite Internet to the world, and more specifically, the people of China. The objective is to emplace a constellation of satellites that would provide secure and uninhibited communications to undermine the Communist Chinese's "Great Fire Wall;" a firewall tightly controlled by the Chinese to manage the information flow entering and leaving its borders.

VOA 2.0 would also be the vehicle to "broadcast" a truthful— much as advocated by Gertz--an honest representation of US core interests and values concerning China. This is not about deception or False-Flag Operations (FFO). It will not create less-than-truthful narratives, (Schultz, 2015), that would undermine the long-term desired outcome of ending Communist China. Any deception operation, if too quickly attempted, would be seen by the average Chinese as propaganda and falsehood. If the US employed it too slowly, the US efforts would appear both inconsistent and insincere. This would not meet the desired outcomes sought. Any effort must be couched in the truth and avoid any hyperbole or partial truths.

> **"Deploy the truth: you cannot win a war if you cannot talk honestly about the enemy,"**
> (Gorka, 2016)

Additionally, a US governmental body would also need to be established—a rebirth of Voice of America via the global Internet[10]. Such an organization would exploit the VOA 2.0 medium and such Internet resources to include social media and open news sources from across the globe. "[Social Media] is a powerful tool with great potential for information warfare" (Gertz, 2017); this method reflects Gertz's own plan to make this a war of ideas. The disruption to the Communist Chinese government's ability to control the information flow to its citizenry would be revolutionary. It would create an open environment that would potentially end Chinese communism similarly to the demise of the former Soviet Union.

Defeating US threats require a new approach to both past strategies and technologies; both will not require armed conflict. They require the avid and thoughtful

---

[10] While the author is no fan of additional bureaucracies, there have been points in US political history where such bodies were effective. This suggestion is based upon the past board's successes in directing the actions of the original VOA.

employment of SCP, through an active IO plan, that holistically dissuades Chinese government hackers, and also their military forces to discontinue any current or future kinetic or virtual attack. VOA 2.0 would be that much needed and more comprehensive core technological solution that would be the primary means to weaken China ideologically.

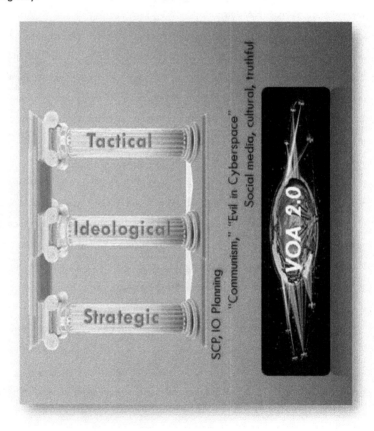

Figure 2. "The Three Pillars"

Defeating an Ideology

So how does the US fight the Chinese Communist ideology? The "second pillar" requires the US to recognize and declare to the world that the ideology of communism is a failed one (*once again*) in any form. It is crucial to

> "It is a key failing of US efforts to fight terrorism that we have not understood the importance of ideology"
> (Gorka & Gorka, 2015, p. 11)

convey this information as was once done regarding a failed former Soviet Union. It can express that failure using ideas transmitted across an open and free Internet. That battle must be executed at the highest levels of the US government to include the communications from the president to the Chinese people directly.

Furthermore, as Reagan designated the Soviet Union, the current Administration should also declare a new "Evil in Cyberspace:" *China*. The confrontation on ideology is not just the identification of enemies but the actual and perceived threats to their preeminence. "In short, the United States has to help defeat an ideology, not just a group of people" (Gorka, 2014).

The Tactical Fight

"Social Media is key to interdiction" (Gorka & Gorka, 2015). This "third" and final component is like how the previous rendition of VOA existed after World

> "The single most effective tool for detecting ISIS supporters is through their social media activity"
> (Gorka & Gorka, 2015, p. 9).

War II. It was to espouse democratic ideas freely across unrestricted airwaves. VOA 2.0 will employ experts in Chinese language and culture to communicate with the Chinese people openly and freely across Facebook, Twitter, Instagram, etc. This effort would require the employment of individuals that can express the truths and failings of the current Chinese communist ideology freely.

The ideas of freedom in a restrictive regime will help shift the Chinese from a centralized and plutocratic government to a preferable free and "democratic" society. While the Chinese Communist Party espouses equality for all, the VOA 2.0 solution would erode the bedrock of this regime. The objective is to ultimately neutralize the government's efforts to quash the exchange of information and ideas freely within China's borders and among its people.

The same tactics, as described earlier by Dr. Gorka: "truthfulness and bringing others into the fight," should be used to defeat the Chinese. Using the same tenets of exploiting social media against ISIS, the US can do the same against the Chinese. It will help accelerate the defeat of China at the tactical through the strategic level by the employment of elements of US power. This would comprise all facets of US power to include primarily the power of information over a genuinely open Internet for the Chinese.

CONCLUSION

As Bill Gertz suggested, the US cannot quietly stand by as the Chinese steal US ideas, innovations, and technologies. It will require a "soft" offensive response through a coordinated message and access to unfettered information by the Chinese people. "Unless we punch back, we will continue to get hit" (Gertz, 2017).

Destroying the Chinese dictatorial "machine" in cyberspace will require attacking them strategically, ideologically, and tactically. The objective is to undermine communism one more time through technological means. Strategically, it will require the US with its allies to deploy global Internet access via the VOA 2.0 solution. It will require an ideological assault on the failures of communism through an open dialog across an open and uncensored Internet. Finally, it will require a tactical communications plan designating China as the premier cyber enemy; doing such will erode their power. It may also result in its near end, much like that demise of the former Soviet Union.

It will be through an active, and non-kinetic cyber actions that will defeat the Chinese ongoing cyber threat to the US and the world. The introduction of a disruptive technological solution, such as VOA 2.0, will provide the Chinese people access to information and knowledge about their repressive government, and much like the end of communism in the former Soviet Union, this is a means to defeat Chinese communism once again in the 21st Century. It potentially will provide the impetus to topple Beijing courtesy of...*cyberspace*.

REFERENCES

Andrew, N., & Scobell, A. (2012). *China's Search for Security*. New York: Columbia University Press.

Applegate, S., Carpenter, C., & West, D. (2017). Searching for Digital Hilltops: A Doctrinal Approach to Identifying Key Terrain in Cyberspace. *Joint Force Quarterly | Issue 84 | 1st Qtr.*, 18-23.

Campbell, C., & Salidjanova, N. (2016, July 12). *South China Sea Arbitration Ruling: What Happened and What's Next?* Retrieved from U.S.-China Economic and Security Review Commission: http://origin.www.uscc.gov/sites/default/files/Research/Issue%20Brief_South%20China%20Sea%20Arbitration%20Ruling%20What%20Happened%20and%20What's%20Next071216.pdf

Collins, K. (2015, September 22). *Chinese leader denies hacks, opens door for cybersecurity accord*. Retrieved from C|NET: https://www.cnet.com/news/chinese-president-denies-hack-attacks-opens-door-for-cybersecurity-accord/

Gertz, B. (2017). *iWar: War and Peace in the Information Age*. New York: Simon and Schuster.

Gorka, S. (2017, January 5). China the True Cyber Threat. (M. Bartiromo, Interviewer)

Gorka, S. L. (2014). Understanding the Enemy. *Special Warfare, Apr-Jun | Volume 27 | Issue 2*, 8-11.

Gorka, S. L. (2016). *Defeating Jihad: The Winnable War*. Washington, DC: Regnery Publishing.

Gorka, S. L., & Gorka, K. C. (2015, November). *ISIS: The Threat to the United States*. Retrieved from Threat Knowledge Group: http://threatknowledge.org/wp-content/uploads/2015/11/TKG-Report_The-ISIS-Threat.pdf

Houck, C. (2017, March 10). *ISIS War Generals to Congress: We Need the State Department*. Retrieved from GovExec: http://www.govexec.com/defense/2017/03/isis-war-generals-congress-we-need-state-department/136062/?oref=river

Iasiello, E. (2012). Is Cyber Deterrence an Illusory Course of Action? *Journal of Strategic Security (7:1)*, 54-67.

Infosec Institute. (2013, October 11). *Hardware attacks, backdoors and electronic component qualification*. Retrieved from Infosec Institute: http://resources.infosecinstitute.com/hardware-attacks-backdoors-and-electronic-component-qualification/

Jaffe, G. (2017, February 20). *For a Trump adviser, An Odyssey from the Fringes of Washington to the Center of Power*. Retrieved from Washington Post: https://www.washingtonpost.com/world/national-security/for-a-trump-adviser-an-odyssey-from-the-fringes-of-washington-to-the-center-of-power/2017/02/20/0a326260-f2cb-11e6-b9c9-e83fce42fb61_story.html?utm_term=.ad57ccb7063b

Joint Chiefs of Staff. (2014, November 20). *Joint Publication 3-13: Information Operations.* Retrieved from Defense Technical Information Center (DTIC): http://www.dtic.mil/doctrine/new_pubs/jp3_13.pdf

Kaplan, F. (2016). *Dark Territory: The Secret History of Cyber War.* New York: Simon and Schuster.

Keys, R., Winstead, C., & Simmons, K. (2010, July 20). *Cyberspace Security and Attribution.* Retrieved from National Security Cyberspace Institute: http://www.nsci-va.org/WhitePapers/2010-07-20-Cybersecurity%20Attribution-Keys-Winstead-Simmons.pdf

Mandiant. (2013, February 18). *APT1: Exposing One of China's Cyber Espionage Units.* Retrieved from Mandiant: http://intelreport.mandiant.com/Mandiant_APT1_Report.pdf

Schultz, R. W. (2015, October 1). *Countering Extremist Groups in Cyberspace.* Retrieved from National Defense University Press | Joint Forces Quarterly | 4th Qtr: http://ndupress.ndu.edu/Media/News/News-Article-View/Article/621124/jfq-79-countering-extremist-groups-in-cyberspace/

US House of Representatives. (2012, October 8). *Investigative Report on the US National Security Issues Posed by Chinese Telecommunications Companies Huawei and ZTE.* Retrieved from https://intelligence.house.gov/sites/intelligence.house.gov/files/documents/Huawei-ZTE%20Investigative%20Report%20(FINAL).pdf

APPENDICES

APPENDIX A- GLOSSARY

Audit log.   A chronological record of information system activities, including records of system accesses and operations performed in each period.

Authentication.   Verifying the identity of a user, process, or device, often as a prerequisite to allowing access to resources in an information system.

Availability.   Ensuring timely and reliable access to and use of information.

Cybersecurity   The process of protecting information by preventing, detecting, and responding to attacks.

Cybersecurity Event   A cybersecurity change that *may* have an impact on organizational operations (including mission, capabilities, or reputation).

Cybersecurity Incident A cybersecurity event that has been determined to have an impact on the organization prompting the need for response and recovery.

Hardware.   The physical components of an information system.
Incident.   An occurrence that actually or potentially jeopardizes the confidentiality, integrity, or availability of an information system or the information the system processes, stores, or transmits or that constitutes a violation or imminent threat of violation of security policies, security procedures, or acceptable use policies.

Information Security.   The protection of information and information systems from unauthorized access, use, disclosure, disruption, modification, or destruction to provide confidentiality, integrity, and availability.

Information System.   A discrete set of information resources organized for the collection, processing, maintenance, use, sharing, dissemination, or disposition of information.

Information Technology. Any equipment or interconnected system or subsystem of equipment that is used in the automatic acquisition, storage, manipulation, management, movement, control, display, switching, interchange, transmission, or reception of data or information by the executive agency. It includes computers, ancillary equipment, software, firmware, and similar procedures, services (including support services), and related resources.

Malicious Code. Software intended to perform an unauthorized process that will harm the confidentiality, integrity, or availability of an information system. A virus, worm, Trojan horse, or other code-based entity that infects a host. Spyware and some forms of adware are also examples of malicious code.

Network. Information system(s) implemented with a collection of interconnected components. Such components may include routers, hubs, cabling, telecommunications controllers, key distribution centers, and technical control devices.

Risk. A measure of the extent to which a potential circumstance or event threaten an entity, and typically a function of (i) the adverse impacts that would arise if the circumstance or event occurs; and (ii) the likelihood of occurrence. Information system-related security risks are those risks that arise from the loss of confidentiality, integrity, or availability of information or information systems and reflect the potential adverse impacts to organizational operations (including mission, functions, image, or reputation), organizational assets, individuals, other organizations, and the Nation.

Security Control. A safeguard or countermeasure prescribed for an information system or an organization designed to protect the confidentiality, integrity, and availability of its information and to meet a set of defined security requirements.

Security Functions. The hardware, software, or firmware of the information system responsible for enforcing the system security policy and supporting the isolation of code and data on which the protection is based.

Threat.   Any circumstance or event with the potential to adversely impact
                               organizational operations (including mission, functions, image, or
                               reputation), organizational assets, individuals, other
                               organizations, or the Nation through an information system via
                               unauthorized access, destruction, disclosure, modification of
                               information, or denial of service.

APPENDIX B- CONTINUOUS MONITORING

Cybersecurity is not about shortcuts. There are no easy solutions to years of leaders demurring their responsibility to address the growing threats in cyberspace. We hoped that the Office of Personnel Management (OPM) breach several years ago would herald the needed focus, energy, and funding to quash the bad-guys. That has proven an empty hope where leaders have abrogated their responsibility to lead in cyberspace. The "holy grail" solution of Continuous Monitoring (ConMon) has been the most misunderstood solution where too many shortcuts are perpetrated by numerous federal agencies and the private sector to create an illusion of success. (See the online article, *Hope for a Holy Grail of Continuous Monitoring*, October 1, 2017, *Signal Magazine* at https://www.afcea.org/content/hope-holy-grail-continuous-monitoring).

Hope for a Holy Grail of Continuous Monitoring
THE CYBER EDGE
October 1, 2017
By Lt. Col. Mark A. Russo, USA (Ret.)

This paper is specifically written to help leaders better understand what constitutes an accurate statement of: "we have continuous monitoring." This is not about shortcuts. This is about education, training, and understanding at the highest leadership levels that cybersecurity is not a technical issue, but a leadership issue.

The Committee on National Security Systems defines ConMon as: "[t]he processes implemented to maintain current security status for one or more information systems on which the operational mission of the enterprise depends," (CNSS, 2010). ConMon has been described as the holistic solution of end-to-end cybersecurity coverage and the answer to providing an effective global Risk Management (RM) solution. It promises the elimination of the 3-year recertification cycle that has been the bane of cybersecurity professionals.

For ConMon to become a reality for any agency, it must meet the measures and expectations as defined in the National Institute of Standards and Technology (NIST) Special Publication (SP) 800-137, Information Security Continuous Monitoring for Federal Information Systems and Organizations. "Continuous monitoring has evolved as a best practice for managing risk on an ongoing basis," (SANS Institute, 2016); it is an instrument that supports effective, continual, and recurring RM assurances. For any agency to indeed espouse it has attained full ConMon compliance, it must be able to coordinate all the described major elements as found in NIST SP 800-137.

ConMon is not just the passive visibility pieces, but also includes the active efforts of vulnerability scanning, threat alert, reduction, mitigation, or elimination of a dynamic Information Technology (IT) environment. The Department of Homeland Security (DHS) has couched its approach to ConMon more holistically. Their program to protect government networks is more aptly called: "Continuous Diagnostics and Monitoring" or CDM and includes a need to react to an active network attacker. "The ability to make IT networks, end-points and applications visible; to identify malicious activity; and, to respond [emphasis added] immediately is critical to defending information systems and networks," (Sann, 2016).

Another description of ConMon can be found in NIST's CAESARS Framework Extension: An Enterprise Continuous Monitoring Technical Reference Model (Second Draft). It defines its essential characteristics within the concept of "Continuous Security Monitoring." It is described as a "...risk management approach to Cybersecurity that maintains a picture of an organization's security posture, provides visibility into assets, leverages use of automated data feeds, monitors effectiveness of security controls, and enables prioritization of remedies," (NIST, 2012); it must demonstrate visibility, data feeds, measures of effectiveness and allow for solutions. It provides another description of what should be demonstrated to ensure full ConMon designation under the NIST standard.

The government's Federal Risk and Authorization Management Program (Fed-RAMP) has defined similar ConMon goals. These objectives are all key outcomes of a successful ConMon implementation. Its "… goal[s]…[are] to provide: (i) operational visibility; (ii) annual self-attestation on security control implementations; (iii) managed change control; (iv) and attendance to incident response duties," (GSA, 2012). These objectives, while not explicit to NIST SP 800-37, are well-aligned with the desires of an effective and complete solution.

RMF creates the structure and documentation needs of ConMon; it represents the specific implementation and oversight of Information Security (IS) within an IT environment. It supports the general activity of RM within an agency. (See Figure 1 below). The RMF "… describes a disciplined and structured process that integrates information security and risk management activities into the system development life cycle" (NIST-B, 2011). RMF is the structure that both describes and relies upon ConMon as its risk oversight and effective mechanism between IS and RM.

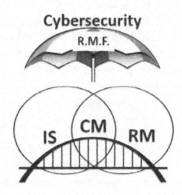

Figure 1. CM "bridges" Information Security and Risk Management

This article provides a conceptual framework to address how an agency would approach identifying a correct ConMon solution through NIST SP 800-137. It discusses the additional need to align component requirements with the *"11 Security Automation Domains"* that are necessary to implement true ConMon. (See Figure 2 below). It is through the complete implementation and

Figure 2. The 11 Security Automation Domains (NIST, 2011)

integration with the other described components—See Figure 3 below--that an organization can correctly state it has achieved ConMon.

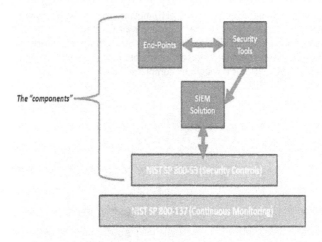

The "components"

Figure 3. The "Components" of an Effective Continuous Monitoring

Continuous Monitoring – First Generation

For ConMon to be effective and genuine, it must align end-point visibility with security monitoring tools. This includes security monitoring tools with connectivity to "end-points" such as laptops, desktops, servers, routers, firewalls, etc. Additionally, these must work with a highly integrated Security Information and Event Management (SIEM) device. The other "component" is a clear linkage between the end-points, security monitoring tools, and the SIEM appliance, working with the *Security Automation Domains* (See Figure 2). These would include, for example, the areas of malware detection, asset, and event management. ConMon must first address these composite components to create a "First Generation" instantiation.

More specifically, a SIEM appliance provides the central core data processing capabilities to expertly coordinate all the inputs and outputs from across the IT enterprise. It manages the data integration and interpretation of all ConMon components. Moreover, it provides the necessary visibility and intelligence for an active incident response capability.

End-point devices must be persistently visible to the applicable security

devices. Together, these parts must align with the respective security controls, as described in NIST SP 800-53. The selected SIEM tool must be able to accept these inputs and analyze them against defined security policy settings, recurring vulnerability scans, signature-based threats, and heuristic/activity-based analyses to ensure the environment's security posture. The outputs of the SIEM must support the further visibility of the IT environment, conduct, and disseminate vital intelligence, and alert leadership to any ongoing or imminent dangers. The expression above is designed to provide a conceptual representation of the cybersecurity professional attempting to ascertain effective ConMon implementation or to develop a complete ConMon answer for an agency. Additionally, the SIEM must distribute data feeds in near-real-time to analysts and key leaders. It provides for multi-level "dashboard" data streams and issues alert based upon prescribed policy settings. Once these base, First Generation functionalities are consistently aligning with the Security Automation Domains, then an organization can definitively express it meets the requirements of ConMon.

End-Points

It is necessary to identify hardware and software configuration items that must be known and constantly traceable before implementing ConMon within an enterprise IT environment. End-point visibility is not the hardware devices, but the baseline software of each hardware device on the network.

Configuration Management is also a foundational requirement for any organization's security posture. Soundly implemented Configuration Management must be the basis of any complete CM implementation. At the beginning of any IS effort, cyber-professionals must know the current "as-is" hardware and software component state within the enterprise. End-points must be protected and monitored because they are the most valuable target for would-be hackers and cyber-thieves.

Configuration Management provides the baseline that establishes a means to identify potential compromise between the enterprise's end-points and the requisite security tools. "Organizations with a robust and effective [Configuration Management] process need to consider information security implications concerning the development and operation of information systems including hardware, software, applications, and documentation," (NIST-A, 2011).

The RMF requires the categorization of systems and data as high, moderate, or low regarding risk. The Federal Information Processing Standards (FIPS) Publication 199 methodology is typically used to establish data sensitivity levels in the federal government. FIPS 199 aids the cybersecurity professional in determining data protection standards of both end-points and the data stored in these respective parts. For example, a system that collects and retains sensitive data, such as financial information, requires a higher level of security. End-points must be recognized as repositories of highly valued data to cyber-threats.

Further, cyber-security professionals must be constantly aware of the "...administrative and technological costs of offering a high degree of protection for all federal systems...," (Ross, Katzke, & Toth, 2005). This is not a matter of recognizing the physical end-point alone, but the value and associated costs of the virtual data stored, monitored, and protected continually. FIPS 199 assists system owners in determining whether a higher level of protection is warranted, with higher associated costs, based upon an overall FIPS 199 evaluation.

Security Tools

Security monitoring tools must identify in near-real-time an active threat. Examples include anti-virus or anti-malware applications used to monitor network and end-point activities. Products like McAfee and Symantec provide enterprise capabilities that help to identify and reduce threats.

Other security tools would address in whole or part the remaining NIST Security Automation Domains. These would include, for example, tools to provide asset visibility, vulnerability detection, patch management updates, etc. However, it is also critical to recognize that even the best current security tools are not necessarily capable of defending against all attacks. New malware or zero-day attacks pose continual challenges to the cybersecurity workforce.

For example, DHS's EINSTEIN system would not have stopped the 2015 Office of Personnel Management breach. Even DHS's latest iteration of EINSTEIN, EINSTEIN 3, an advanced network monitoring and response system designed to protect federal governments' networks, would not have stopped that attack. "...EINSTEIN 3 would not have been able to catch a threat that [had] no known footprints, according to multiple industry experts" (Sternstein, 2015).

Not until there are a much higher integration and availability of cross-cutting intelligence and more capable security tools, can any single security tool ever be fully effective. The need for multiple security monitoring tools that provide "defense in depth" may be a better protective strategy. However, with multiple tools monitoring the same Security Automation Domains, such an approach will undoubtedly increase the costs of maintaining a secure agency IT environment. A determination of Return on Investment (ROI) balanced against a well-defined threat risk scoring approach is further needed at all levels of the federal IT workspace.

Security Controls

"Organizations are required to adequately mitigate the risk arising from the use of information and information systems in the execution of missions and functions" (NIST, 2013). This is accomplished by the selection and implementation of NIST SP 800-53, Revision 4, described security controls. (See Figure 4 below). They are organized into eighteen families to address sub-set security areas such as access control, physical security, incident response, etc. The use of these controls is typically tailored to the security categorization by the respective system owner relying upon FIPS 199 categorization standards. A higher security categorization requires the more significant implementation of these controls.

Security Information and Event Management (SIEM) Solutions

The SIEM tool plays a pivotal role in any viable "First Generation" implementation. Based on NIST and DHS guidance, a capable SIEM appliance must provide the following functionalities:

- "Aggregate data from "across a diverse set" of security tool sources;
- Analyze the multi-source data;
- Engage in explorations of data based on changing needs
- Make quantitative use of data for security (not just reporting) purposes including the development and use of risk scores; and
- Maintain actionable awareness of the changing security situation on a real-time basis" (Levinson, 2011).

"Effectiveness is further enhanced when the output is formatted to provide information that is specific, measurable, actionable, relevant, and timely" (NIST, 2011). The SIEM device is the vital core of a full solution that collects, analyzes, and alerts the cyber-professional of potential and actual dangers in their environment.

Several major SIEM solutions can effectively meet the requirements of NIST SP 800-137. They include products, for example, IBM® Security, Splunk®, and Hewlett Packard's® ArcSight® products.

For example, Logrhythm ® was highly rated in the 2014 SIEM evaluation. Logrhythm® provided network event monitoring and alerts of potential security compromises. The implementation of an enterprise-grade SIEM solution is necessary to meet growing cybersecurity requirements for auditing of security logs and capabilities to respond to cyber-incidents. SIEM products will continue to play a critical and evolving role in the demands for "...increased security and rapid response to events throughout the network" (McAfee® Foundstone Professional Services®, 2013). Improvements and upgrades of SIEM tools are critical to providing a more highly responsive capability for future generations of these appliances in the marketplace.

Next Generations

Future generations of ConMon would include specific expanded capabilities and functionalities of the SIEM device. These second generation and beyond evolutions would be more effective solutions in future dynamic and hostile network environments. Such advancements might also include increased access to a greater pool of threat database signature repositories or more expansive heuristics that could identify active anomalies within a target network.

Another futuristic capability might include the use of Artificial Intelligence (AI). Improved capabilities of a SIEM appliance with AI augmentation would further enhance human threat analysis and provide for more automated responsiveness. "The concept of predictive analysis involves using statistical methods and decision tools that analyze current and historical data to make predictions about future events..." (SANS Institute). The next generation would boost human response times and abilities to defend against attacks in a matter of milli-seconds vice hours.

Finally, in describing the next generations of ConMon, it is not only imperative to expand data, informational, and intelligence inputs for new and more capable SIEM products, but that input and corresponding data sets must also be thoroughly vetted for completeness and accuracy. Increased access to signature and heuristic activity-based analysis databases would provide a more significant risk reduction. More significant support from private industry and the Intelligence Community would also be significant improvements for Agencies that are continually struggling against a more-capable and better-resourced threat.

ConMon will not be a reality until vendors and agencies can integrate the right people, processes, and technologies. "Security needs to be positioned as an enabler of the organization—it must take its place alongside human resources, financial resources, sound processes and strategies, information technology, and intellectual capital as the elements of success for accomplishing the mission," (Caralli, 2004). ConMon is not just a technical solution. It requires capable organizations with trained personnel, creating effective policies and procedures with the requisite technologies to stay ahead of the growing threats in cyberspace.

Figure 6 below provides a graphic depiction of what ConMon components are needed to create a holistic NIST SP 800-137-compliant solution; this demonstrates the First-Generation representation. Numerous vendors are describing that they have the "holy grail" solution, but until they can prove they meet this description in total, it is unlikely they have a complete implementation of a thorough ConMon solution yet.

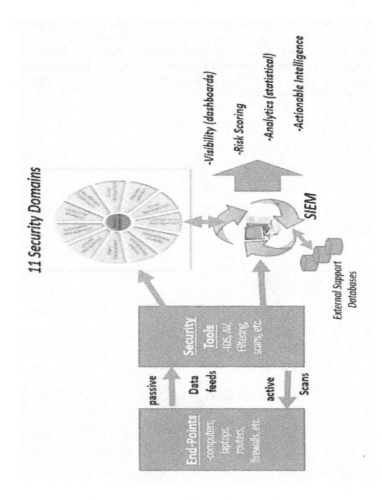

Figure 6. First Generation Continuous Monitoring

Endnotes for "Continuous Monitoring: A More Detailed Discussion"

Balakrishnan, B. (2015, October 6). *Insider Threat Mitigation Guidance*. Retrieved from SANS Institute Infosec Reading Room: https://www.sans.org/reading-room/whitepapers/monitoring/insider-threat-mitigation-guidance-36307

Caralli, R. A. (2004, December). *Managing Enterprise Security (CMU/SEI-2004-TN-046)*. Retrieved from Software Engineering Institute: http://www.sei.cmu.edu/reports/04tn046.pdf

Committee on National Security Systems. (2010, April 26). *National Information Assurance (IA) Glossary*. Retrieved from National Counterintelligence & Security Center: http://www.ncsc.gov/nittf/docs/CNSSI-4009_National_Information_Assurance.pdf

Department of Defense. (2014, March 12). *DOD Instructions 8510.01: Risk Management Framework (RMF) for DoD Information Technology (IT)*. Retrieved from Defense Technical Information Center (DTIC): http://www.dtic.mil/whs/directives/corres/pdf/851001_2014.pdf

GSA. (2012, January 27). *Continuous Monitoring Strategy & Guide, v1.1*. Retrieved from General Services Administration: http://www.gsa.gov/graphics/staffoffices/Continuous_Monitoring_Strategy_Guide_072712.pdf

Joint Medical Logistics Functional Development Center. (2015). JMLFDC Continuous Monitoring Strategy Plan and Procedure. Ft Detrick, MD.

Kavanagh, K. M., Nicolett, M., & Rochford, O. (2014, June 25). *Magic Quadrant for Security Information and Event Management*. Retrieved from Gartner: http://www.gartner.com/technology/reprints.do?id=1-1W8AO4W&ct=140627&st=sb&mkt_tok=3RkMMJWWfF9wsRolsqrJcO%2FhmjTEU5z17u8lWa%2B0gYkz2EFye%2BLIHETpodcMTcVkNb%2FYDBceEJhqyQJxPr3FKdANz8JpRhnqAA%3D%3D

Kolenko, M. M. (2016, February 18). *SPECIAL-The Human Element of Cybersecurity*. Retrieved from Homeland Security Today.US: http://www.hstoday.us/briefings/industry-news/single-article/special-the-human-element-of-cybersecurity/54008efd46e93863f54db0f7352dde2c.html

Levinson, B. (2011, October). *Federal Cybersecurity Best Practices Study: Information Security Continuous Monitoring.* Retrieved from Center for Regulatory Effectiveness: http://www.thecre.com/fisma/wp-content/uploads/2011/10/Federal-Cybersecurity-Best-Practice.ISCM_2.pdf

McAfee® Foundstone® Professional Services. (2013). *McAfee.* Retrieved from White Paper: Creating and Maintaining a SOC: http://www.mcafee.com/us/resources/white-papers/foundstone/wp-creating-maintaining-soc.pdf

NIST. (2011-A, August). *NIST SP 800-128: Guide for Security-Focused Configuration Management of Information Systems.* Retrieved from NIST Computer Security Resource Center: http://csrc.nist.gov/publications/nistpubs/800-128/sp800-128.pdf

NIST. (2011-B, September). *Special Publication 800-137: Information Security Continuous Monitoring (ISCM) for Federal Information Systems and Organizations.* Retrieved from NIST Computer Security Resource Center: http://csrc.nist.gov/publications/nistpubs/800-137/SP800-137-Final.pdf

NIST. (2012, January). *NIST Interagency Report 7756: CAESARS Framework Extension: An Enterprise Continuous Monitoring Technical Reference Model (Second Draft),.* Retrieved from NIST Computer Resource Security Center: http://csrc.nist.gov/publications/drafts/nistir-7756/Draft-NISTIR-7756_second-public-draft.pdf

NIST. (2013, April). *NIST SP 800-53, Rev 4: Security and Privacy Controls for Federal Information Systems.* Retrieved from NIST: http://nvlpubs.nist.gov/nistpubs/SpecialPublications/NIST.SP.800-53r4.pdf

Ross, R., Katzke, S., & Toth, P. (2005, October 17). *The New FISMA Standards and Guidelines Changing the Dynamic of Information Security for the Federal Government.* Retrieved from Information Technology Promotion Agency of Japan: https://www.ipa.go.jp/files/000015362.pdf

Sann, W. (2016, January 8). *The Key Missing Piece of Your Cyber Strategy? Visibility.* Retrieved from Nextgov: http://www.nextgov.com/technology-news/tech-insider/2016/01/key-missing-element-your-cyber-strategy-visibility/124974/

SANS Institute. (2016, March 6). *Beyond Continuous Monitoring: Threat Modeling for Real-time Response.* Retrieved from SANS Institute: http://www.sans.org/reading-room/whitepapers/analyst/continuous-monitoring-threat-modeling-real-time-response-35185

Sternstein, A. (2015, January 6). *OPM Hackers Skirted Cutting-Edge Intrusion Detection System, Official Says.* Retrieved from Nextgov: http://www.nextgov.com/cybersecurity/2015/06/opm-hackers-skirted-cutting-edge-interior-intrusion-detection-official-says/114649/

APPENDIX C - HUAWEI SENIOR STAFF BIOGRAPHIES

The following biographical information on Huawei's board of directors and the supervisory board comes from the 2010 annual report posted on Huawei's corporate website (huawei.com) unless otherwise noted.

Board of Directors

Sun Yafang

Born: Sun's date of birth is unknown, but a *Xinjing Bao* report indicates that she is in her fifties (28 October 2010)
Education: Chengdu University of Electronic Science and Technology
Joined Huawei: 1989

In 1982, Sun was employed as a technician by Xinfei TV Manufacturers. Beginning in 1985, she worked as an engineer for the Beijing Research Institute of Communication Technology. Since joining Huawei in 1989, she has served as an engineer with the Marketing and Sales Department, president of the Procurement Department, president of the Human Resources Committee, president of the Business

Sun Yafang (孙亚芳)
Chairwoman

Photos: Huawei official website; big5.xinhuanet.com/gate/big5/news.xinhuanet.com/fortune/2011-01/19/c_12998438.htm

Transformation Executive Steering Committee, president of Strategy and Marketing, and president of Huawei University. She has served as the chair of the board of directors since 1999. Huawei's 2010 annual report does not mention that Sun, the most trusted deputy of Huawei's founder Ren Zhengfei (*Xinjing Bao*, 28 October 2010), once worked for the PRC Ministry of State Security, a detail reported in Chinese media which has reinforced suspicions over potential close links between Huawei and the Chinese Government.

- *Xinjing Bao* reported that Sun worked for the Communications Department of the Ministry of State Security for an unspecified period before joining Huawei (28 October 2010).

- The same 28 October *Xinjing Bao* report also said that Sun joined Huawei in 1992 instead of 1989, as stated on Huawei's website.

- An undated report on *Feng Huang Wang* stated that Sun used her "connections" at the Ministry of State Security to help Huawei through financial difficulties "at critical moments" when the company was founded in 1987.

Ren Zhengfei

Born: 25 October 1944 to parents who were middle school teachers, Ren spent his primary and middle school years in a remote, mountainous village in Guizhou Province. *Education*: In 1963, he began his collegiate studies at the Chongqing Institute of Civil Engineering and Architecture (CICEA). However, the overseas edition of party daily *Renmin Ribao* reported that Ren graduated from Chongqing University of Posts and Telecommunications instead of the CICEA (1 December 2010). *Founded Huawei*: 1987

Ren Zhengfei (任正非)
Founder, CEO, Deputy Chairman

Photos: Huawei official website; news.xinhuanet.com/fortune/2010-12/01/c_12833931.htm

Upon graduation, Ren was employed by an unspecified civil engineering organization until 1974, when he enlisted in the PLA Engineering Corps as a soldier participating in the construction of the French-imported *Liao Yang Chemical Fiber Factory*, where he successively held technician and engineer positions and was promoted to deputy director, which was a civilian title equivalent to a deputy regimental chief without a military rank.

As a result of his outstanding performance at work, he was invited to attend the National Science Conference in 1978 and the 12th National Party Congress in 1982. Ren retired from the military in 1983 when the Chinese Government disbanded the entire Engineering Corps. Consequently, he worked for the logistics service base of the Shenzhen South Sea Oil Corporation (SSSOC). When he grew dissatisfied with his work at the SSOC, Ren decided to establish Huawei in 1987 with an initial registered capital of RMB 21,000 (US$5,675). In 1988, he became the CEO of Huawei and had held the position since.

Chinese media have portrayed Ren as the most influential business leader in China, as well as a tenacious and dedicated leader who seldom mentions his military background in public.

- In April 2011, the Chinese version of Fortune Magazine, *Forbes China*, listed Ren as China's most influential business leader.

- *Ta Kung Pao*, a PRC-owned Hong Kong daily, reported that Ren is a "tough," "low-profile," and "dedicated" leader who attaches great importance to "discipline" and "obedience" at work (25 April 2011).

Guo Ping

Born: 1966
Education: MS from Huazhong University of Science and Technology (HUST)
Joined Huawei: 1988

Guo has served as an R&D project manager, general manager of supply chain, director of the Executive Office, chief legal officer, president of the Business Process and IT Management Department, president of the Corporate Development Department, chairman and president of Huawei Device, corporate executive vice president (EVP), and chairman of the Finance Committee.

Guo Ping (郭平)
Deputy Chairman

Photos: Huawei official website;
sz.bendibao.com/news/2011420/297068.htm

An undated posting on *Former Huawei Employees Community* [Qian Huawei Ren Shequ], a forum registered in Beijing and hosted by former and current Huawei employees, indicated that after meeting Ren for the first time at HUST, Guo was employed as a product manager and later became the company's chief recruiter at the university (exhwren.com).

Chinese media reports depict Guo Ping as a "low-profile" and "level-headed" manager leading Huawei's US team, who emerged victorious from a lawsuit with Cisco.

- In 2003, Guo traveled to the United States and directed Huawei's US team to "turn the tables" on Cisco after the US company accused Huawei of copying software and patent infringement, according to a 13 March 2010 report in *21 Shiji Jingji Baodao*, a Guangzhou-based economy-focused daily.

Xu Zhijun

Born: 1967
Education: Ph.D. from Nanjing University of Science and Technology
Joined Huawei: 1993

Xu has served as president of Huawei's wireless product line, chief strategy and marketing officer, chief products and solutions officer, corporate executive vice president, and chairman of the Investment Review Board.

PRC media has quoted Xu as saying that Huawei will seek to make inroads in the US market despite opposition from the US Government.

Xu Zhijun (Eric Xu, 徐直军)
Deputy Chairman

Photo sources: Huawei official website; tech.sina.com.cn/other/2004-08-05/1429398879.shtml

- Xu said that the company would continue to try to crack the US market despite opposition from the US Government, according to a 28 January 2011 report in *Shanghai Diyi Caijing Ribao,* a financial daily also known as *Chinese Business News*.

- The same 28 January report also cited Xu as saying that Huawei would first seek to establish business connections with non-mainstream telecom operators in the United States, gradually expand its outreach to third-tier or second-tier operators, and finally do business with top operators.

Hu Houkun

Birth: Unknown
Education: Huazhong University of Science and Technology
Joined Huawei: 1990

Hu has held several senior roles within Huawei including president of Huawei's Chinese Market, president of Huawei Latin America, president of the Global Sales Department, chief sales and service officer, chief strategy and marketing officer, chairman of the Corporate Global Cyber Security Committee, chairman of Huawei USA, corporate executive vice president, and chairman of the Human Resources Committee.

Hu Houkun
(Ken Hu, 胡厚崑) *Deputy Chairman*

Photo sources: Huawei official website; it.sohu.com/20110225/n279522552.shtml

In February 2011, Hu wrote a letter to the US Government following Huawei's failed attempt to acquire 3Leaf in the United States.

* On 25 February 2011, following Huawei's failure to acquire US server vendor 3Leaf, Hu sent a letter to the US Government challenging US Government claims ranging from the company's involvement with the Chinese Government to Huawei's policies toward intellectual property rights and licensing regulations, according to a 25 February 2011 report on China National Radio (CNR), a Chinese state-run overseas broadcaster.

* The same 25 February report cited Hu as saying that his company did receive financial support from the Chinese Government for research and development activities but that this is consistent with the level of government financial support provided to other businesses in China and many other countries, including the United States.

Meng Wanzhou

Born: Unknown
Education: MS from Huazhong University of Science and Technology in 1998
Joined Huawei: 1993

Meng Wanzhou
(Cathy Meng, 孟晚舟)
Executive Director

Photo source: Huawei official website

Meng, Ren Zhengfei's daughter, has served as director of the International Accounting Department, chief financial officer (CFO) of Huawei Hong Kong, president of the Accounting Management Department, president of the Sales Financing and Treasury Management Department. Currently, she concurrently serves as the executive director of the Board of Directors and the CFO of Huawei.
Meng reportedly holds a Ph.D., and Chinese media report she is likely to succeed Ren Zhengfei as Huawei's CEO.

- *Zhongguo Jingying Bao* reported that Meng is the daughter of Huawei founder Ren Zhengfei and holds a Ph.D. from Nankai University (29 April 2011).

- A 19 April 2011 report in *Zhengquan Ribao* notes that Ren has been grooming Meng to be the company's CFO since she joined Huawei in 1993, and she is likely to succeed Ren in due course.

Xu Wenwei

Born: 1963
Education: MS from Southeast University in 1990
Joined Huawei: 1991
Xu has served as president of the International
Technical Sales and Marketing Department, president
of the European Region, chief strategy and marketing
officer, chief sales and service officer, president of the
Joint Committee of Regions. He currently also serves
as president of the Enterprise Business Group.
According to a 19 April 2011 report in *Zhengquan
Ribao,* Xu is the husband of Meng Wanzhou.

Xu Wenwei (William Xu, 徐文伟)
Executive Director

Photo sources: Huawei official website;
cnii.com.cn/20030915/ca202487.htm

Li Jie

Born: 1967
Education: MS from Xi'an Jiao Tong University
Joined Huawei: 1992
Li has served as president of an unspecified region, president of
the
Global Technical Service Department, president of the Human
Resource Department, and president of the Joint Committee of
Regions.

Li Jie (Jason Li, 李
杰) *Executive
Director*

Photo source: Huawei
official website

Ding Yun

Born: 1969
Education: MS from Southeast University
Joined Huawei: 1996

Ding has served as president of Product Line, president of the Global Solution Sales Department, president of the Global Marketing Department, and chief products and solutions officer.

Ding Yun (Ryan Ding, 丁耘) *Executive Director*

Photo sources: Huawei official website; sh.eastday.com/qtmt/20100925/u1a804411.html

Chen Lifang

Born: Unknown
Education: Northwest University
Joined Huawei: 1995

Chen has served successively as the chief representative of the
Beijing Representative Office, vice president of the International Marketing Department, deputy director of the Domestic Marketing Management Office, president of the Public Affairs and Communications Department, and corporate senior vice president.

Chen Lifang (陈黎芳)

Director

Photo source: Huawei official website

Wan Biao

Born: 1972
Education: BS from University of Science and Technology of China
Joined Huawei: 1996

Wan has served as director of the UMTS RAN System, president of the UMTS Product Link, president of the Wireless Product Line, and CEO of Huawei Device.

Wan Biao (万飚)

Director

Photo sources: Huawei official website; maigoo.com/maigoocms/2011/0706/kjmrwb.html

Zhang Ping' an

Born: 1972
Education: MS from Zhejiang University
Joined Huawei: 1996

Zhang has served as president of Product Link, senior vice president, vice president of strategy and marketing, regional vice president, vice president of the Global Technical Service, and CEO of Huawei Symantec.

Zhang Ping'an (Alex Zhang, 张平安)

Director

Photo sources: Huawei official website; http://tech.sina.com.cn/other/2009-11-28/16563633017.shtml

Yu Chengdong

Born: 1969
Education: MS from Tsinghua University
Joined Huawei: 1993
Yu has served as director of 3G Products, vice president of the Wireless Technical Sales Department, president of the European Region, and chief strategy and marketing officer.

Yu Chengdong (Richard Yu, 余承东)

Director

Photo sources: Huawei official website; tech.ifeng.com/telecom/special/huawei-sunyafang/content-1/detail_2010_11/17/3134909_0.shtml

Supervisory Board

Liang Hua

Born: 1964
Education: Ph.D. from Wuhan University of Technology
Joined Huawei: 1995

Liang has served as president of the Supply Chain Management Department, CFO of Huawei, and president of the Global Technical Service Department.

Liang Hua (梁华)

Chairman of the Supervisory Board

Photo source: Huawei official website

Peng Zhiping

Born: 1967
Education: MS from Fudan University *Joined Huawei*: 1996

Peng has served as president of the Terminal Product Link, president of the Optical Network Product Link, president of the Supply Chain Management Department, vice president of the Procurement Qualification Management Department. Currently, he also serves as chief operations and delivery officer.

Peng Zhiping (Benjamin Peng, 彭智平) *Member of the Supervisory Board*

Photo sources: Huawei official website; customs.gov.cn/publish/portal0/tab35021/info 191274.htm

Ren Shulu

Born: 1956
Education: Yunnan University
Joined Huawei: 1992

Ren has served as president of Shenzhen Smartcom Business Co., Ltd, president of the Internal Service Management Department, and head of the Capital Construction Investment Management Committee. On 19 April 2011, *Zhengquan Ribao* reported that Ren Shulu was elected to Huawei's supervisory board for the first time in January 2011. He is the brother of Ren Zhengfei, according to the same article.

Ren Shulu (Steven Ren, 任树录)
Member of the Supervisory Board

Photo source: Huawei official website

Tian Feng

Born: 1969
Education: BS from Xi'an University of Electronic Science and Technology
Joined Huawei: 1995

Tian has served as regional vice president, regional president, and CEO of Huawei Agisson.

Tian Feng (田峰)
Member of the Supervisory Board

Photo source: Huawei official website

Deng Biao

Born: 1971
Education: BS from Jiangxi University *Joined Huawei*: 1996

Deng has served as president of the Access Network Product Link, president of the Network Product Line, and CEO of Huawei Software Technologies Co., Ltd.

Deng Biao (邓飚)

Member of the Supervisory Board

Photo sources: Huawei official website; tech.sina.com.cn/t/2006-12-06/09561274135.shtml

About the Author

Mr. Russo is an internationally published author, and his work has been published in four foreign languages in addition to English. He is a former Senior Information Security Engineer within the Department of Defense's (DOD) F-35 Joint Strike Fighter program. He has an extensive background in cybersecurity and is an expert in the Risk Management Framework (RMF) and DOD Instruction 8510, which implements RMF throughout the DOD and the federal government. He holds both a Certified Information Systems Security Professional (CISSP) certification and a CISSP in information security architecture (ISSAP). He holds a 2017 certification as a Chief Information Security Officer (CISO) from the National Defense University, Washington, DC. He retired from the US Army Reserves in 2012 as the Senior Intelligence Officer.

Credentials:

Mr. Russo holds a current Intelligence Fundamentals Professional Certification (IFPC) that was developed to accomplish the goal set forth by the Under Secretary of Defense for Intelligence (USD(I)) to professionalize the defense intelligence workforce. The IFPC has established a common standard of the fundamental knowledge and skills expected of all who currently serve in and support, and those who hope to serve in and support, the DoD Intelligence Enterprise (DIE). The IFPC is based on cross-cutting and enterprise-wide Defense Intelligence Fundamentals standards, which depict the core expectations of what all Defense Intelligence Professionals, regardless of Service/Agency, Function/Specialty and experience level, must know and be able to do to successfully execute and contribute to the execution of intelligence missions, functions, and activities at the fundamental level. The IFPC will also serve to ensure incoming defense intelligence professionals meet knowledge standards.

To earn the IFPC, you must meet all eligibility requirements and pass the 90-item IFPC exam. The certification lasts for three years and may be renewed by retaking/passing the IFPC exam or achieving a higher-level certification from a program endorsed by the USD(I).

He is the former CISO at the Department of Education, wherein 2016; he led the effort to close over 95% of the outstanding US Congressional and Inspector General cybersecurity shortfall weaknesses spanning as far back as five years.

Mr. Russo is the former Senior Cybersecurity Engineer supporting the Joint Medical Logistics Development Functional Center of the Defense Health Agency (DHA) at Fort Detrick, MD. He led a team of engineering and cybersecurity professionals protecting five major Medical Logistics systems supporting over 200 DOD Medical Treatment Facilities around the globe.

In 2011, Mr. Russo was certified by the Office of Personnel Management as a graduate of the Senior Executive Service (SES) Candidate program.

From 2009 through 2011, Mr. Russo was the Chief Technology Officer at the Small Business Administration (SBA). He led a team of over 100 IT professionals in supporting an intercontinental Enterprise IT infrastructure and security operations spanning 12-time zones; he deployed cutting-edge technologies to enhance SBA's business and information sharing operations supporting the small business community. Mr. Russo was the first-ever Program Executive Officer (PEO)/Senior Program Manager in the Office of Intelligence & Analysis at Headquarters, Department of Homeland Security (DHS), Washington, DC. He was responsible for the development and deployment of secure Information and Intelligence support systems for OI&A to include software applications and systems to enhance the DHS mission. He was responsible for the program management development lifecycle during his tenure at DHS.

He holds a Master of Science from the National Defense University in Government Information Leadership with a concentration in Cybersecurity and a Bachelor of Arts in Political Science with a minor in Russian Studies from Lehigh University. He holds Level III Defense Acquisition certification in Program Management, Information Technology, and Systems Engineering. He has been a member of the DOD Acquisition Corps since 2001.

Check out these Cybersecurity Books at Amazon by the Author

The Agile/Security Development Life Cycle (A/SDLC): Integrating Security Functionality into the SDLC ~SECOND EDITION

https://www.amazon.com/Agile-Security-Development-Life-Cycle/dp/1794490574/ref=tmm_pap_swatch_0?_encoding=UTF8&qid=1555271578&sr=8-1-fkmrnull

In this **SECOND EDITION of THE AGILE SECURITY DEVELOPMENT LIFE CYCLE (A/SDLC),** we expand and include new information to improve the concept of "Agile Cyber." We further discuss the need for a Security Traceability Requirements Matrix (SecRTM) and the need to know where all data elements are located throughout your IT environment to include Cloud storage and repository locations. The author continues his focus upon ongoing shortfalls and failures of "Secure System Development." The author seeks to use his over 25 years in the public and private sector program management and cybersecurity to create a solution. This book provides the first-ever integrated operational-security process to enhance the reader's understanding of why systems are so poorly secured. Why have we, as a nation, missed the mark in cybersecurity? Why nation-states and hackers are successful daily? This book also describes the two-dominant mainstream "agile" NIST frameworks that can be employed and how to use them effectively under a Risk Management approach. We may be losing "battles, " but maybe it is time we genuinely commit to winning the cyber-war.

The Threat Hunt Process (THP) Roadmap: A Pathway for Advanced Cybersecurity Active Measures

ACTIVELY MONITOR, DISSUADE, AND DEFEAT THE CYBER THREAT IN YOUR IT ENVIRONMENTS. This is a book for advanced cybersecurity personnel and does demand additional resources to support its implementation. This book is designed to implement the most extensive Threat Hunt Process (THP) for companies and agencies seeking to proactively determine whether intrusions into their Information Technology (IT) environments are real and malicious. THP is the active ability for businesses or organizations to investigate, mitigate, and stop the "bad guys" in their tracks. How do you select, collect, align, and integrate THP data and information for tracking daily operations and overall organizational security? How do you reduce the effort in THP activities to get problems solved? How can you ensure that plans include every THP task and that every possibility is considered and responded to by the Incident Response Team? How can you save time investigating and responding to strategic and tactical threats with limited resources? This book is designed to help you create a compelling and repeatable THP. Mr. Russo has worked the grassroots challenges of cyberspace throughout his detailed and extensive public and private sector security career. He will guide you based on a proven track record of answers to better understand and implement THP solutions efficiently and rapidly.